RESPONSIVE ARCHITECTURE: MOODY•NOLAN RECENT WORK

Morris Newman

First Edition
© 2008 Morris Newman

No part of this book may be
reproduced in any manner
without written permission
except in the case of brief
quotations embodied in
critical articles and reviews.

Published in the United States of
America in 2008 by Balcony Press.

For information address
Balcony Media, Inc.
512 E. Wilson Avenue, Suite 213
Glendale California 91206.

Design by DISTINC
Printing and production by
Navigator Cross-Media
Printed in South Korea

Library of Congress
Control Number: 2008925942
ISBN 978-1-890449-46-9

Introduction

RESPONSIVE ARCHITECTURE

It is comparatively easy to create a work of architecture that is good-looking and nothing more. Far more difficult is creating a building that we can imagine ourselves inhabiting, even if we have never seen it in real life, let alone been inside of it. In the case of the Harrisburg National Museum of African American History, we find ourselves experiencing this kind of empathy with a building that was never actually constructed. If we can figure out why the museum project excites this response in us, we may be at least one step closer to understanding the architecture of Moody·Nolan.

The centerpiece of the African American history museum is a pair of 19th century buildings, one of which was a boarding house for prominent members of the African American community, and the other a funeral parlor. With their brownstone façades and narrow windows, these prim,

University of Illinois at Chicago West Campus Sports and Fitness Facility Addition/Renovation Chicago, IL	*2006 Citation of Excellence Award, Learning by Design* *2006 Innovative Architecture and Design Award, Recreation Management* *2005 Design Excellence, National Organization of Minority Architects (NOMA)*	*2005 Merit Award for Addition/Renovation, American Institute of Architects (AIA), Ohio Chapter*

unsmiling buildings seem foreboding, as if they came out of a painting by Edward Hopper. Surrounding these buildings, but not smothering them, is a new curtain wall of glass with wavy forms that make the curtainwall look like a linen sheet billowing in the breeze. In contrast to the forbidding look of the old funeral parlor, the new building is all about transparency — "the movement from darkness to light," according to architect Curtis J. Moody, FAIA — in which we can see a jazz club, and probably hear the band, too, from behind that glass wall, which now seems to balloon and subside with the phrasing of a tenor sax solo. Even from the experiential distance of an artist's rendering, it is possible to imagine oneself standing outside the museum or even venturing inside, if the band is having a good night.

The ability of certain buildings to spark an imaginative response in us, to the point of imagining ourselves inside particular spaces in those buildings, recalls an observation by Robert J. Yudell in his article, "Body Movement," included in the book, *Memory and Architecture*. Yudell argues for architecture that relates to human experience and human movement. For Yudell, the best buildings are those that evoke what he calls a "body response," essentially an imaginative response to a building that seems to offer the possibility of physical movement: "We can imagine scaling, leaping, and occupying its surfaces and interstices," he writes.

Transparency is one of the chief means by which Curtis Moody and his design associates at Moody·Nolan achieve this sense of body response. This quality of literal transparency is very similar to the kind famously achieved by Herman Hertzberger in his Central Beheer office building (1972), in which the typically hermetic spaces of office work become open for all to see, on multiple levels, all at once. For Hertzberger, transparency was a means to introduce a sense of democracy inside a building type that otherwise tends toward the hierarchal. For Moody, the use of a similar kind of transparency at The Ohio State University Recreation and Physical Activity Center (RPAC) is the means to achieve a sense of partic-

---

Left
Harrisburg National Museum of African American History Design Competition
Harrisburg, PA

Right
The Ohio State University Recreation and Physical Activity Center (RPAC)
Columbus, OH

2008 Association of College Unions International, Facility Design Award

2007 AIA Ohio, Merit Award for Newly Completed Buildings, Additions, Remodelings, Renovations, Restorations

2007 National Organization of Minority Architects, Honor Award

2007 Athletic Business Magazine, Facility of Merit

2007 Recreation Management, Innovative Architecture and Design Award

2007 National Intramural Recreation Sports Association, Outstanding Indoor Sports Facilities

ipation, even a sense of belonging. In the student center, on which Moody·Nolan collaborated with design architect Antoine Predock, the ability to see the full array of exercise and athletics makes the building into something like a visual essay in the variety of sports: Entering into the front lobby, we can immediately see three levels of activity, including a large room on the basement level of students on treadmills. In another area, we find ourselves walking opposite a stack of three glass-walled basketball courts that become living theaters of furious movement. Each window is a blur of elbows, sweatbands and flying hair. For student athletes, a group of dark, solitary spaces have become linked into a single, public building with a communal feeling. For the student seeking a warm place to walk in the midst of an Ohio winter, the building may serve either as entertainment or as a quiet place to open a book.

The Ohio State University
Recreation and Physical
Activity Center (RPAC)
Columbus, OH

Moody likes to call the work of his firm "responsive architecture." Here, the word responsive must be understood in a variety of senses. The plainest meaning, of course, is that Moody·Nolan is responsive to its clients' visions, and that an anxious developer can get Curt on the telephone. That is important for an entrepreneurial practice like Moody·Nolan, which must continually prove its worth in a business world often indifferent to any concept of architecture beyond the serviceable. Responsive, however, also has other meanings, such as the ability to respond architecturally to the circumstances presented by a particular site, and to lift the serviceable into the realm of Signature architecture.

Moody·Nolan's approach to landscape is not dissimilar to its ideas about transparency: The goal is always to serve the end user, either through expanding the view or improving mobility. At the Youngstown City Schools East High School in Youngstown, Ohio, the dramatic, circular elevation might have been justifiable on aesthetic grounds alone, but Moody·Nolan rarely pursues an aesthetic solution that is unrelated to the quality of experience of the end user. The half-circular portion of the building pushes forward toward the forest, stepping down the natural slope in three terraces. Those "steps" are echoed in the roofline. The architects have fitted clerestory windows in the vertical surfaces of these steps to provide panoramic views of the forest, while delivering natural light to the interior. The formal exercise of the elevation, in short, is grounded in providing views and daylighting, simply because the architect saw the opportunity for both.

An even more dramatic response to landscape is the Baker University Center at Ohio University which straddles a steep hillside. One side of the building is a historicist building with a tower and two two-story wings; the other side, on the lower side of the hill, is a five-story contemporary building with occasional flourishes of historical detail. To break up the mass of this enormous multi-purpose building, Moody·Nolan has shaped the enve-

Youngstown City Schools
East High School
Youngstown, OH

lope into what appears to be a grouping of historical buildings. And to activate retail space on upper stories, they proposed something never before seen in exurban Athens, Ohio: A set of four-story escalators to carry visitors up the multiple flights of stairs that would otherwise be too formidable for retail and other active public uses. This building is now the bridge connecting upper and lower ends of the campus, with students traveling through the building at all times of year. With its combination of scales and styles, in particular its skillful variation between strict and abstracted forms of historicism, this complex building has now become the standard for all future buildings on the campus.

Ohio University
Baker University Center
Athens, OH

2008 Association of College
Unions International, Facility
Design Award

2008 Grand Prize,
Learning by Design

A more subtle adaptation to landscape can be found in the Tom Muehlenbeck Center, a community recreation complex in Plano, Texas, that incorporates an existing creek into both the land planning and the architecture. The curving elevation of the center, an elongated S shape in plan, parallels the natural path of the creek, while the creek itself provides a natural boundary to the courtyard in front of the building. And again, Moody• Nolan seizes an opportunity for a display of literal transparency, even within the limited confines of a two-story interior, where a curving walkway cuts through the front lobby. In another nod to natural surroundings, the outer glass wall of Ithaca College's New Athletics and Events Center in Ithaca, New York, a more subtle gesture toward the surrounding outdoors, is covered with an abstract representation of trees. Like real trees, this wall provides passive cooling by shielding the interior from direct sunlight.

Tom Muehlenbeck Center
Plano, TX

*2008 Recreation Management,
Innovative Architecture and
Design Award*

Ithaca College
New Athletics
and Events Center
Ithaca, NY

**Cincinnati Public Schools
School for Creative and
Performing Arts (SCPA)**
Cincinnati, OH

Modern Contextualism

Moody·Nolan's adaptability to conditions extends to urban conditions, even those that seem tough or uninviting. Perhaps the most remarkable illustration of the firm's wholehearted commitment to contextual design can be seen in the pair of extremely different schemes that Moody·Nolan prepared for the Cincinnati Public Schools School for Creative and Performing Arts in Cincinnati's downtown area. (The firm served as design architect for the collaborative project.) In the first scheme, the owner had chosen a site containing a historic building, Moody and his associates plunged into designing a multi-building complex in a historicist style. Despite the remarkable end result, the owners decided to locate the school several blocks away in an old industrial neighborhood. Moody·Nolan responded to the site change with a completely different scheme, this time in a hard-edged idiom that is similar to the earlier scheme only in its insistence on granting each function, even the box office, with its own characteristic shape and structure. The auditorium is expressed as a simple rotunda, which is given extra importance through a cladding of stainless-steel shingles set in a continuous diaper pattern.

Moody·Nolan's feeling for context is strong enough to enable the firm to take a further step and create context—that is, to introduce buildings and landscape into undeveloped areas to serve as a reference point for future architects to build on. A subtle example is the Jackson State University Student Union in Jackson, Mississippi. The building serves as the eastern gateway of the campus, while demarcating the campus from its urban surroundings. Moody·Nolan marks the importance of the gateway location with a sensitively scaled plaza that opens directly off the new walkway. The courtyard sits at an angle to the walkway, to maintain its identity as a distinct space.

In some settings, creating context means supplying a needed element to a particular site where that element is lacking. Windows were one thing that

Cincinnati Public Schools School for Creative and Performing Arts (SCPA), Cincinnati, OH

Historic contextualism

2002 Honor Award, National Organization of Minority Architects (NOMA)

was lacking from a cluster of research buildings on the campus of Purdue University in West Lafayette, Indiana. As if to compensate for the lack of windows, the new Wayne T. and Mary T. Hockmeyer Hall features glass volumes that seem almost to tumble out of their red-brick masonry frames.

Yet another example of Moody·Nolan supplying context where it was previously lacking is the remarkable parking structure in the Arena District in downtown Columbus. While few parking structures qualify as architecture, the exception is the Nationwide Mutual Insurance Company Parking Garage, a flamboyant, red-brick structure that supplies the excitement for a home-town game by itself. Through the use of supergraphics, billboards, a glass stair tower and a street-level façade divided into bays resembling store windows, the parking structure soars up the street, and establishes a big-city image for this evolving district, which remains only partly developed.

In the foregoing list of projects, Moody·Nolan has shown that it has more than enough firepower to be considered a design architect, and take its place among the national firms that can vie for the most significant jobs requiring signature design. The firm has long since earned the "Q's" (as in qualifications) to do virtually any kind of project. In Moody·Nolan's first 25 years of operations, the firm has designed the full gamut of commercial and institutional buildings: office buildings, affordable housing, high-rise residential towers, university buildings, sports facilities, health care, retail and other specialized building types. Few architects have this range of work tucked under their belts.

Moody has handled his career as an entrepreneur, not as an academic. As a designer with artistic ambition, he might have had an easier time teaching while keeping a boutique firm for the chance to build an avant-garde house or two that could find its way into well-read shelter magazines. But Moody is an organization builder by temperament. In doing so, he has chosen perhaps the most difficult route, the vertical ascent, to a

---

Left
Jackson State University Student Center
Jackson, MS

Right
Smith Brothers Hardware Renovation
Columbus, OH

1999 James B. Recchie Design Award, Columbus Landmarks Foundation

2000 Honor Award, American Institute of Architects, Columbus Chapter

career in architecture. Moody opened the firm in 1982 alone as Moody and Associates, later teaming up with Howard Nolan in 1984. The practice started in an old house in a transitional neighborhood, with the bath tub serving as an ad-hoc cabinet for drawings. In this do-or-die phase of an architectural career, artistic ambition takes the back seat to survival, as young architects bid on every job, glamorous or not, that comes into view. And many of the jobs they managed to get in those early years did not encourage creativity, Moody recalls: "We had developers come in here telling us, 'this is the building, this is how it lays out, it will be red brick and seventy-five percent glass.' And we tried as hard as we could to put some quality into the building."

Persistence has its rewards. In 25 years, the firm has opened seven offices in six states, is licensed in 18, and has designed projects in more than 40 states. The current headquarters is located on the edge of the Arena District in downtown Columbus, Ohio, which Moody·Nolan designed and of which Moody is part owner.

Beyond business development, the firm has developed a consistent design ethos centered on humane values, and has pursued those values within the limits—sometimes very constrained limits—of the work that has come through the door. Moody·Nolan has embraced the notion of responsive architecture as a mode of inquiry. My prediction for the second 25 years of Moody·Nolan? Design excellence, combined with responsiveness in all of its connotations will greatly enlarge the national reputation of this home-grown firm.

Left
Ithaca College
New Athletics and
Events Center
Ithaca, NY

2006 Honor Award, National
Organization of Minority
Architects (NOMA)

Right
Nationwide Mutual Insurance
Company Parking Garage
Columbus, OH

2000 Design Excellence Award,
National Organization of
Minority Architects

Chapter 1

COMPOSITION

More than any other single document, the plan is the signature document of an architect. As any first-year instructor in architecture will tell you, everything flows from the plan: composition, spaces, even the choice of materials. A quick glance at the plan by any architect says much about his or her compositional style, as well as his or her priorities.

The priority in the plans of Moody·Nolan is to make the organization of the building readily apparent to its users. Each space, wherever possible, is given a very distinct footprint and geometry. This distinctness is less motivated by ideas of pure form than a concern for the experience of the end user. On its face, this claim seems unremarkable, because nearly every architect asserts that his or her buildings have been designed for the well-being of the client and the betterment of the built environment. The only

Ithaca College
New Athletics and
Events Center
Ithaca, NY

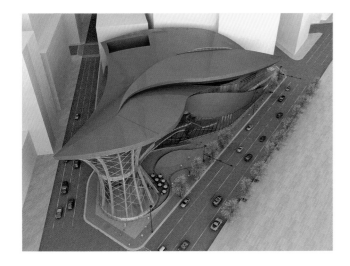

Pittsburgh African American Cultural Center Design Competition
Pittsburgh, PA

2008 Merit Award for Unbuilt Projects, American Institute of Architects (AIA)

difference here is that in Moody·Nolan's case, the claim is true: A discipline that runs throughout the firm is a concern first and foremost about how things look and feel on the ground, as opposed to the way things look to birds in the air, worms in the ground, architectural photographers or magazine lay-out editors. This concern for the experience of the people who will actually use the buildings, however, may not be readily apparent to some until the plan materializes into a completed building.

This concern for the end user is particularly true in public facilities designed by Moody·Nolan. In these projects, the planning tends to assign a distinct shape and volume for each major space—giving the plans a clarity bordering on bubble-diagrams. The extreme clarity is intended as a tool for wayfinding, so that a large and complex building can be navigated with a single glance at the plan, or understood and remembered after a single walkthrough. The plan for the Kress Events Center at the University of Wisconsin–Green Bay, for which Moody·Nolan served as Design Architect in association with Venture Architects, is an overt example of using geometry to give distinctive identity to major spaces. The program was to remodel a portion of an existing building, while adding another 41,000 square feet for a new event space, team lockers and a training room. The oval addition, which stretches toward campus, is a direct reflection—an upward extrusion—of the oval jogging track located along the periphery of the oval form. The result is a façade animated by the image of people in motion. It gets dark early in Green Bay, and it's often cold, but any time of day, one sees people running through that oval. In the center of the oval, the floor drops away, providing the joggers with the view of other people exercising on lower levels in the building.

Movement and wayfinding is the informing principle behind the plan for the Columbus Police Academy, one of the firm's earliest public commissions. Here, circulation has largely determined the shape and programming of the building, which is essentially a doughnut surrounding a

**University of
Wisconsin–Green Bay
Kress Events Center**
Green Bay, WI

circular green space. In layout, the building is a single-loaded corridor, that is, a single glass-lined hallway facing the garden, with major spaces opening off the corridor. The original architectural intent was to encourage the cadets and their instructors to take shortcuts through the courtyard.

Planning, obviously, is a multi-purpose discipline. Beyond pure programmatic organization and circulation, the plan must also help the building find its feet on the ground. The footprint of the Ithaca College New Athletics and Events Center in Ithaca, New York has a curved shape reflecting the hilly topography of upstate New York, as well as the outcroppings of rock marking the landscape. Half the building sits directly on a bed of granite, a condition dramatized by the field-stone wall at the base of the building, as well as the stone path that leads into the building and continues through the lobby. In the case of the Tom Muehlenbeck Center in Plano, Texas, the planning takes its cue from a difficult condition, which is a river and riparian habitat that cuts the park in half, limiting its usefulness. Moody·Nolan's solution was to make the bisecting river into an "event," by pushing public spaces up to the river, rather than turning away from it. The positive reception to these newly defined outdoor spaces between the rec center and the river bank has created interest in further developing the area with an outdoor amphitheatre, according to the project architect.

Internal planning and site planning come together in buildings that Moody·Nolan's architects have designed as public courtyards. At the Student Union at Jackson State University in Jackson, Mississippi, the building serves both as a kind of marker or gateway for the east boundary of the campus, while accenting that boundary with a courtyard fashioned as an L-shaped plan. Another courtyard-making building is Wayne T. and Mary T. Hockmeyer Hall at Purdue University in West Lafayette, Indiana. Given a program for both lab spaces (which research scientists often prefer to be dark, for no good reason) and administrative spaces (which employees often prefer to have lots of natural light, but which are often dark), the

Previous Page
**University of
Wisconsin–Green Bay
Kress Events Center**
Green Bay, WI

Columbus Police Academy
Columbus, OH

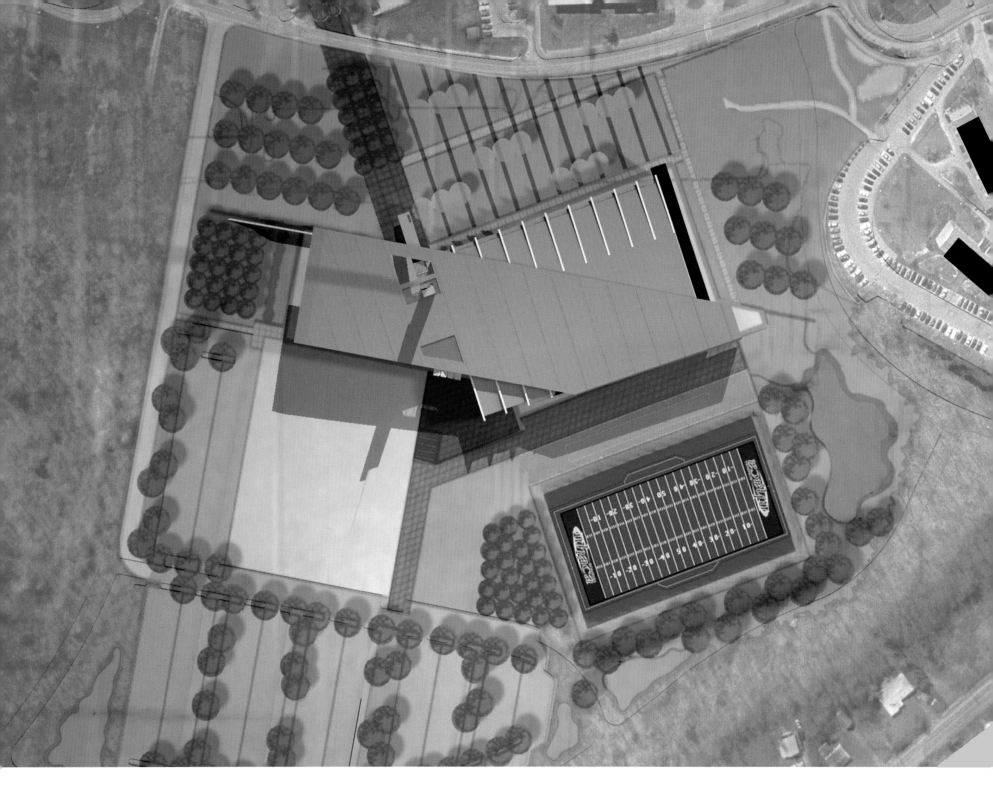

**Ithaca College
New Athletics and
Events Center**
Ithaca, NY

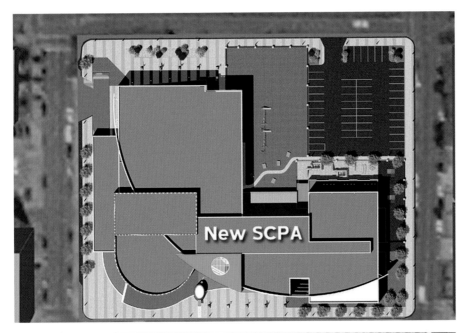

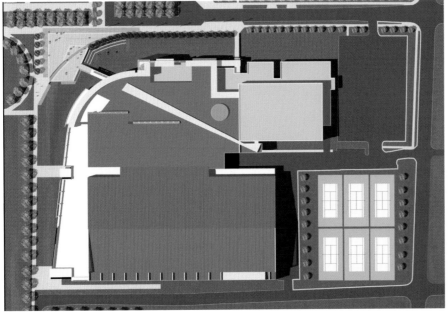

Above
**Cincinnati Public Schools
School for Creative and
Performing Arts (SCPA)**
Cincinnati, OH

Below
**University of Akron
Student Recreation Center
& Field House**
Akron, OH

Jackson State University
Student Center
Jackson, MS

project architect took the dichotomy of the program to pull the two functions apart, and create a courtyard between them. The labs are located behind a wall of brick and windows with translucent glass. The administrative spaces are located on the other side of the U-shaped courtyard, in which curved glass volumes seem to spring exuberantly forward in the elevation, "like a banana being unpeeled," in the words of the project architect. I wonder whether the regents of Purdue University saw the potential for light and movement in the plans of the Hockmeyer Hall, when first proposed. When the building is complete, however, the potential for movement in the "unpeeling banana" of the plan will be plain for all to see.

Purdue University
Wayne T. & Mary T.
Hockmeyer Hall
West Lafayette, IN

Chapter 2

MASSING

Moody·Nolan practices a communicative type of architecture. Whenever possible, the façade and even the shape of buildings are communication devices encoded with narratives for end users. This use of massing-as-message is notably helpful in large public buildings, which the firm designs with the intent to assist people in orientation and wayfinding.

There are few mysteries as to where different spaces are located in the Cincinnati Public Schools School for Creative and Performing Arts, one of the firm's most extroverted and sculptural designs. The style of the building is described as "constructivist and slightly edgy," by the project architect, and the allusion to Russian Constructivism makes particular sense for this building, which looks like an assemblage of separate, self-

Cincinnati Public Schools
School for Creative and
Performing Arts (SCPA)
Cincinnati, OH

Wayne State University
Student Center
Detroit, MI

contained pieces. The drum-shaped, 750-seat auditorium is clearly visible as an individual volume from the street. The auditorium, meanwhile, hovers above a glass-lined lobby, clearly the most public space in the complex. The narrow marquee stretches in front of the auditorium like a piece of fabric hurriedly yanked in front of the building, as if to hide the connection between the performance space above and the lobby below. The box office, in the shape of truncated cone, emerges from the elevation almost as a building in itself: This arresting, "light tower," clad in internally lit orange panels and bearing a Kleig-strength spotlight on its head (in the original scheme), seems slightly extraterrestial, as if communicating with ticket buyers beyond the stars. On the edges of the building, the squarish, red-brick façades mimic the aging buildings of downtown Cincinnati. The school of performing arts, in short, is a performance in itself.

Moody·Nolan's use of massing as an aid to wayfinding is particularly useful in massive complexes like student unions and field houses, which must accommodate the constant movement of a large number of people, day and night. The strongest example to date is the new Wayne State University Student Center near downtown Detroit. The plan of this enormous building could be crudely described as a dumbbell, with two major activity centers on either end connected by retail-lined circulation. In a gesture signifying pedestrian movement, a sharp-edged mass crashes like an arrow through the western wall. If students have not yet grasped the meaning of that symbol, they can get the message of circulation even more literally, by the sight of people on exterior catwalks on the second level.

Animating the elevation with human movement is a favorite device of Moody·Nolan, which seems to take every opportunity to display people at work, or in motion or simply walking through its buildings. The massing of the Wayne T. and Mary T. Hockmeyer Hall at Purdue University in West Lafayette, Indiana, is largely inspired by the idea of transparency (surrounding buildings are windowless). Here, the architects at

Wayne State University
Student Center
Detroit, MI

Moody·Nolan have located glass-lined hallways on the front façade of the building, including exterior catwalks on the second and third levels, as if to express the unconscious urge of students in the Purdue University life-sciences campus to escape their windowless warrens and breathe fresh air.

If Moody·Nolan's use of massing can help users manage complexity, massing can also be used to accent a building, giving it an unusual presence on the street. In the case of the Columbus State Community College Discovery Exchange, a glass-covered entrance kiosk stands almost as a separate, intimately scaled portico or entrance hall on the edge of an otherwise conventional retail building. This simple gesture of making a small portico to a much larger building, which is a device that Moody·Nolan has repeated on several occasions, here gives the building a public feeling appropriate for this downtown college campus; glass is invariably a symbol of public life and participation in the symbolic language of the firm.

**Columbus State
Community College
Discovery Exchange**
Columbus, OH

**Columbus State
Community College
Discovery Exchange**
Columbus, OH

University Hospitals
Twinsburg Health Center
Twinsburg, OH

University Hospitals
Twinsburg Health Center
Twinsburg, OH

St. Elizabeth Hospital
Boardman Campus
Youngstown, OH

Rather than narrate the movement of people, the New Athletics and Events Center at Ithaca College in Ithaca, New York, helps us visualize the movement of warm air as it rises. Designed for an environmentally minded client on a wooded campus in upstate New York, the massing of this enormous field house is an exercise in impassive-solar cooling; the building is eligible for LEED Silver certification. The slight chevron shape of the front elevation acts as a kind of wind scoop to capture prevailing breezes. The upward tilt of the ceiling, meanwhile, parallels the movement of the air as it floats upward toward a thermal chimney, a 140-foot tower that could be described as a slightly abstracted campanile. The ceiling is covered by a flat sheet of steel cladding. That cladding continues uninterruptedly into the interior of the thermal tower, as if the steel surfaces were tracing the invisible movement of air. In short, the New Athletics and Events Center is a demonstration of the great promise for architecture produced from the marriage of sustainability and visual imagination. The Ithaca College building in particular suggests that climate will once again become the source of dramatic gestures in architecture.

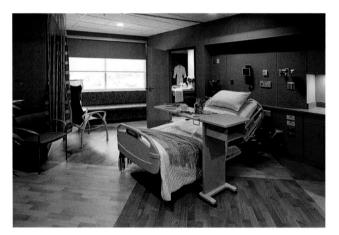

St. Elizabeth Hospital
Boardman Campus
Youngstown, OH

Chapter 3

TRANSPARENCY

In their oft-quoted essay, "Transparency: Literal and Phenomenal," Colin Rowe and Robert Slutsky identified two different kinds of transparency in architecture. The first is literal transparency, which is transparency in the ordinary, see-through sense of the word. The second type, however, involves a "simultaneous perception of different spatial locations." An easier way of saying the same thing, perhaps, is that perceived transparency presents the illusion of a series of overlapping layers. In a way, this second kind of transparency could be likened to *trompe l'oeil* in painting, in that it creates an illusion of space on a two-dimensional surface.

Few buildings embody the idea of perceived transparency more clearly than The Ohio State University at Marion Library and Classroom Building. This complex is an important addition to the university: It is an

The Ohio State University at Marion Library and Classroom Building
Marion, OH

1996 Design Excellence Award, National Organization of Minority Architects (NOMA)

**University of
Wisconsin–Green Bay
Kress Events Center**
Green Bay, WI

"image" facility intended to represent both the university's commitment to education as well as community outreach. (Residents of the nearby city of Marion share library privileges with Ohio State students.) Accordingly, the university has given the library a highly visible position on the edge of a pond, making the building look all the more magisterial through reflections on the water. Using the pond as a reflecting pool is a nod to International Style Modernism, which borrowed the idea, in turn, from certain kinds of traditional architecture, such as the reflecting pools of Mughal palaces in India.

At the center of the composition is an enormous rotunda, which seems haunted by the ghost of the Italian architect, Aldo Rossi, who repopularized the use of rotundi in architecture in the 1970s and '80s, in his attempt to reintroduce some ancient building types back into modern architecture. In Moody·Nolan's library, the rotunda has massive centrality; it is clear the entrance and the "center" of the building, even though the rotunda sits a bit off-center to the rest of the building. From this rotunda, two wings emerge from either side, like spokes attached to a hub. The short wing, nearly windowless, is reserved for computer labs. The longer wing, on the opposite side of the rotunda, has many windows and contains classrooms and library space.

This long library wing becomes the occasion for a virtuoso display of layering, in the form of a "forced" perspective: The bottom three stories, which push forward from the façade, are clad in masonry panels with "punched" windows. In an inventive move that furthers the illusion of receding plains in a way that again recalls *trompe l'oiel,* a row of five columns at the edge of the building step down in height, which enhances the illusion of receding space. Adding a further illusion of depth to the elevation are a set of glass curtain walls, each framed in masonry that also appear to step back into an illusory perspectival space.

Moody·Nolan's skillfully managed illusion of space at The Ohio State library building is an atypical approach for the firm, which generally opts

**The Ohio State University
at Marion Library and
Classroom Building**
Marion, OH

for more straightforward effects. One aspect of the library elevation—the interplay of masonry against glass—can be found throughout the firm's work. Now, façades that contrast solid panels against transparent or translucent glass are extremely common in commercial architecture. What makes many of the elevations by Moody·Nolan different and more interesting, however, is a consistent symbolism in layering, with masonry consistently symbolizing the outer, protective wall, while glass symbolizes the interior of the building, and as such, represents the inner personality, which is more vulnerable and more human than the building's hard, masonry frame. In some cases, the glass seems to burst forth from the interior of buildings, to dramatic effect, creating a dramatic, even disconcerting sense of inner becoming outer, and vice versa.

The game of Masonry-outside/glass-inside is one of the favorite expressive devices in Moody·Nolan's tool bag. By opposing contrary elements, Moody·Nolan's architects are often able to spin narratives about their buildings, their purposes and their end users. In some cases, the dialogue of glass and brick can be read as a comment on the activity that takes place inside particular buildings. Moody·Nolan's innovation, in short, has been to use the everyday materials of commercial construction to create a poetic metaphor for architecture, an art that is concerned simultaneously with the relationship of inner and outer.

Glass seems subordinate to the building as a whole at the Hampton University Student Center in Hampton, Virginia, where glass surfaces are ecessed behind protective-looking masonry frames in the front elevation. Those frames serve, in part, as sun screens. This elegantly detailed and proportioned elevation is one of the firm's finest.

Glass becomes slightly more assertive, if still subordinate, at the Columbus State Community College Discovery Exchange. Here, the glass entrance portico seems a like a beacon of friendliness against the flat, largely opaque façade of the retail portion of the building. A billboard-

---

Previous pages 50-51
University of Akron
Student Recreation Center
& Field House
Akron, OH

Previous pages 52-53
The Ohio State University
at Marion Library and
Classroom Building
Marion, OH

Hampton University
Student Center
Hampton, VA

Hampton University
Student Center
Hampton, VA

Ohio University
Baker University Center
Athens, OH

Ohio University
Baker University Center
Athens, OH

**The Ohio State University
Recreation and Physical
Activity Center (RPAC)**
Columbus, OH

shaped window pokes out of the elevation of the otherwise conventional retail building, as if to wave hello to students in the streets of this urban campus setting.

Windows take on an even bolder personality in other buildings, such as the Wayne T. and Mary T. Hockmeyer Hall on the Purdue University campus in West Lafayette, Ind. Here, in a building devoted to molecular biology, glass seems to lose its dependence on the brick exoskeleton, leaping forward from the masonry frame like an unexpectedly high ocean wave. It is tempting to interpret this façade as an allegory of molecular research, where

Ohio University
Baker University Center
Athens, OH

**University of
Wisconsin–River Falls
University Center**
Riverfalls, WI

Previous Page
**The Ohio State University
Recreation and Physical
Activity Center (RPAC)**
Columbus, OH

Above
**Arena Park Place
Feasibility Study**
Columbus, OH

the normally sub-microscopic realm of biochemistry emerges from invisibility to become something large and important in this academic setting.

Another project where glass represents strength is the competition project for the Harrisburg National Museum of African American History. The inventively folded curtain wall challenges, and wins, dominance over the comparatively opaque masonry buildings on either side of it. The notion of modern glass architecture winning out over repressive-looking Victorian masonry reflects the museum's theme of light triumphing over darkness.

And in the Arena Park Place condominium tower proposed for the North Market area of downtown Columbus, the glass has shed nearly all of its masonry, except for a few shreds that cling to the sides of the building, as if to serve as mere symbols of cladding, rather than actually covering the building. In a residential tower intended for young professionals working in downtown Columbus, transparency represents freedom, coupled with a subliminal sense of personal display. Arena Park Place is an example of literal tansparency pushed to its limits. Glass has come to envelop the entire building, while brick has become purely ornamental. The triumph of transparency does not end the story, however. The cycle will begin again with future buildings that have their own stories to tell.

Arena Park Place
Feasibility Study
Columbus, OH

The Ohio State University
Recreation and Physical
Activity Center (RPAC)
Columbus, OH

Chapter 4

SECTION

Students walking on the West Chicago campus of the University of Illinois do not merely see the new Student Recreation Center; they have an active encounter with it. Although the main portion of the building is off the side of a busy pedestrian path, the third story of the rec center juts out from the building, hovering directly above the foot path like a giant tree branch with windows. As the students step within sight of the cantilevered structure, they are treated to a glimpse of other students exercising on stationary bicycles and other equipment through large windows.

People-watching, as it turns out, is a two-way street: Those inside the building are entertained by the sight of fellow students parading by two stories below. Unlike the old rec center, which was dark and inward-look-

Ithaca College
New Athletics and
Events Center
Ithaca, NY

ing, the new Student Recreation Center goes out of its way to be social and engaging and, above all, to be visible.

The transformation of the UIC West Campus Sports and Fitness Facility from a hidden cavern to an exciting public area is characteristic of Moody·Nolan's approach to the design of interior spaces. Those are best understood in cross-sectional views, because the section is the design document that best reveals both the spatial qualities of buildings and the ways those spaces relate to the surrounding world.

The section is also a good way to gain a fuller appreciation for one of the best abilities of Moody·Nolan: its concern for maximizing views into buildings from the outside. This is the aspect of "responsive" architecture that responds to the end user. Here, architecture addresses the basic human need (or curiosity) to peer inside hidden spaces and peek at the human activity occurring within.

The emphasis on visual contact between those inside buildings with those outside serves purposes both aesthetic and humanistic. Aesthetically, opening the elevation with large, street-level windows is a way of integrating the human body into the elevation. On the functional side, the ability to see inside buildings is also a way of making those buildings participate more fully in the life of a larger community, such as a university campus. And, as we note elsewhere, a building that can be "read" from the outside can also assist in wayfinding, especially when visitors can actually see their intended destination from the outside.

Moody·Nolan's emphasis on the mutual visibility between people on the interior of buildings and those outside is also a strategy to animate architecture, that is, to make human beings an intrinsic part of the way that buildings look and feel. Just as Bishop Berkeley, the 18th century philosopher, believed that the world would cease to exist if God were not looking at it continuously, Moody·Nolan seems to operate with the assumption that spaces do not exist unless people are actively looking into them and

University of Illinois at Chicago East Campus Student Recreation Facility
Chicago, IL

2007 Athletic Business Magazine, Facility of Merit

Previous Page
University of Illinois
at Chicago West Campus
Sports and Fitness Facility
Addition/Renovation
Chicago, IL

University of Akron
Student Recreation Center
& Field House
Akron, OH

out of them at the same time. This visual interaction is one of the firm's methods to shape, and hopefully enlarge, the experience of those who use their buildings, as well as those who simply walk by them.

The inventiveness of Moody•Nolan's design work on the West Chicago campus of the University of Illinois, mentioned above, demonstrates the firm's commitment to mutual visibility. Interestingly, Moody•Nolan did not set out to create a dramatic cantilever. Instead, the cantilever grew out of a more mundane solution to expand the floor space inside the recreation center without enlarging the building's original footprint. The solution was to enlarge the size of upper floors through the use of cantilevers that extended over all four sides of the building. The most notable cantilever, which stretches 12 feet over a public walkway, is the longest and most daring. The decision to make this cantilever virtually a glass box was a happy inspiration later in the design process. In addition to the sight of people inside, people on the ground can also see a patch of sky through the windows of the rec center. The opaque building works hard at being transparent.

Moody•Nolan's major sports facilities excel in mutual visibility. The new fitness room the firm added to the Kress Events Center at the University of Wisconsin-Green Bay contains jogging tracks within a glass-walled perimeter. The center is a prominent object on the campus, with an oval shape emerging like a seed pod from the outer walls of Kress. Green Bay gets dark early in the evening, and the design team thought the campus would benefit from this glowing, ovoid lantern filled with joggers and runners. The runners themselves have the benefit of looking down to a "sunken" exercise area on a lower floor, and this view relieves the tedium of jogging.

In other sports facilities, the use of a running track becomes the device that opens multi-story views to joggers, such as at the Student Recreation Center and Field House at the University of Akron in Akron, Ohio, where a third-story track threads through the enormous building like a catwalk

University of Akron
Student Recreation Center
& Field House
Akron, OH

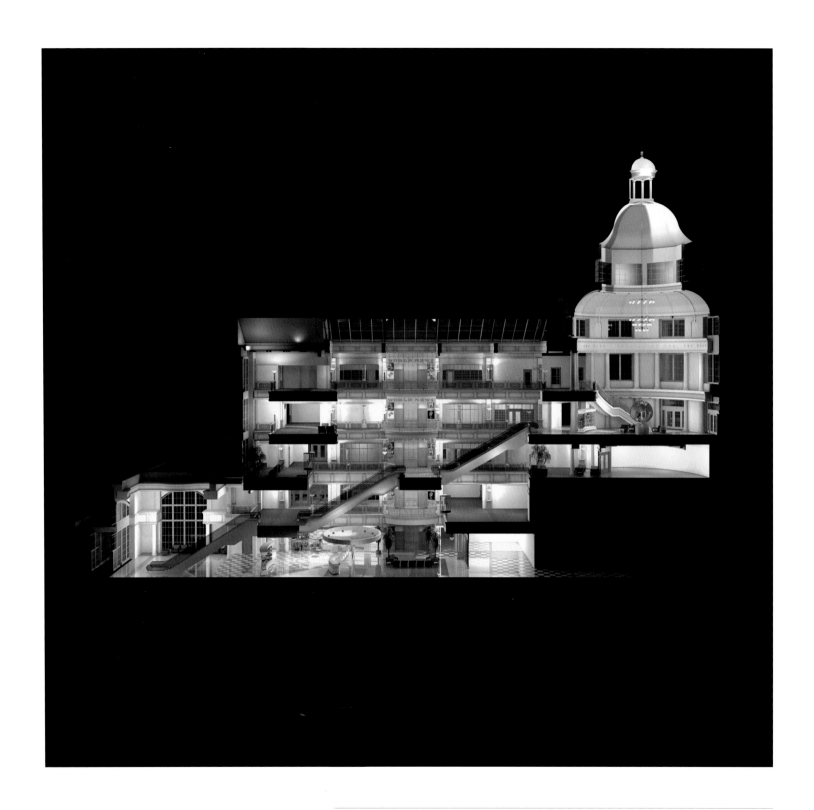

Ohio University
Baker University Center
Athens, OH

suspended in space, offering vertiginous, two-story views below the feet of joggers.

The effect of looking down onto a vast space is achieved to spectacular effect at Ithaca, where the architects make use of the natural slope of the site by locating the entrance at grade while nestling the enormous field house at the lower level. (This lower level roughly corresponds to the base of the slope.) Visitors enter the stone-lined lobby at grade, shortly to arrive at a dramatic view of the field house, the floor of which is located 30 feet below the lobby level. The view opens up suddenly, almost unexpectedly as if it were a chasm in the earth. This simple but powerful example of spatial design, that of providing a penetrating view through a building, stirs up powerful responses similar to our reactions to open landscape.

**University of
Wisconsin–Green Bay
Kress Events Center**
Green Bay, WI

Chapter 5

ELEVATION

When asked about the future stylistic direction of Moody·Nolan, principal Curtis J. Moody points to the Wayne State University Student Center in Detroit, Michigan. This long, horizontal building is non-traditional in the extreme: Jagged and asymmetrical, the student union is a playful composition on the idea of construction: The entire building appears to be four or five smaller buildings that have been neatly, if eccentrically, put together, assembled by a giant carpenter, who pieced the thing together by cutting notches in some buildings, then sliding other buildings into those cuts, where they fit exactly. The sum of all these parts is a building both sculptural and expressive, particularly the west side of the elevation, which terminates in a sharp edge like an axe blade. Daringly, the entire cantilevered form is supported by a single concrete column.

Wayne State University
Student Center
Detroit, MI

Time Warner Cable
Mid-Ohio Division
Columbus, OH

Freewheeling as it may appear, the façade of the student union is also a communication device that tells observers how to use the building. We have already seen that Moody·Nolan designs public buildings to make them easily used by the public. At the WSU Student Center, the two drums or rotundas on either end of the student union are clearly recognizable as major public areas and destination points. The emphatic horizontal gesture that runs down the center of the elevation and terminates in the axe head, meanwhile, symbolizes the central hallway in the building. The façade, to a certain degree, is a diagram of the internal spaces, meant to be understood at a glance.

Moody·Nolan does not always use complex forms to express complex buildings. For the regional headquarters of Time Warner in downtown Columbus, the firm adopted the coolness and restrained imagery favored by Corporate America. Powerful and understated at the same time, this minimalist composition seems to broadcast a message of corporate unity and discipline. Glass, the symbol of public life in many of Moody·Nolan's buildings, is here concentrated in the center, to indicate the public areas of the building: the lobby and the elevator cores.

Again, as we saw in the discussion on massing, the firm often chooses to break up the façades of large buildings into a village-like arrangement of "mini-buildings," each expressing an individual element of the program. The most developed example of the village approach is the School for Creative and Performing Arts in downtown Cincinnati, where each element of the program—the theater, the ticket booth, even the marquee—has its own distinct form.

The Pittsburgh African American Cultural Center, a competition project, is another example of Moody·Nolan dividing the elevation into several distinct forms as a means to tell visitors how to navigate through the building. Making a rare departure from abstraction, Moody·Nolan here uses the literal form of an African drum as the entrance pavilion. This

Time Warner Cable
Mid-Ohio Division
Columbus, OH

hourglass-shaped pavilion is a variation on the hour-glass-shaped *tama* and *djembe* drums of Senegal. The wings of the museum, covered in a curving curtain wall of steel and glass, might be seen as the arms of an African dancer with wind billowing through his sleeves. At the same time, the Pittsburgh museum has the same understood-at-a-glance quality as the Wayne State Student Center: The drum-shaped pavilion is clearly the entrance, while long, ribbon-like windows, which seem to unfurl from the glass of the entrance pavilion, give us a preview of the exhibition spaces. This elevation is probably Moody·Nolan's most innovative and explorative.

Equally symbolic, or nearly so, is the elevation of the competition project for the Harrisburg National Museum of African American History, where, as we saw before, the transparent glass façade symbolizes light, while the heavy, opaque masonry of historic buildings on either side of the façade symbolize darkness and oppression.

Another important aspect of Moody·Nolan's elevations, however, is not indicated in the plans: the presence of people. Across the 200-foot length of the WSU Student Center we can see people in motion on the three-story stairwell and strolling on an external walkway directly beneath the aforementioned "axe blade" on the west end of the building. We also see them standing on balconies and verandas scattered across the façade. For all of its artistry, the most significant aspect of the WSU Student Center may be the importance of the human form in the composition. Every person who has visited a Classical building or a Gothic cathedral will be aware that the human form was an integral part of architecture in prior ages. Among other things, the presence of life-size statuary helped lend buildings a sense of human scale, while providing a way to measure buildings, using the height of one's own body as a mental yardstick. The presence of the human form in architecture also resulted in buildings that more closely resembled the human body; The symmetrical arrangement of

Previous Page
Cincinnati Public Schools
School for Creative and
Performing Arts (SCPA)
Cincinnati, OH

Pittsburgh African American
Cultural Center
Design Competition
Pittsburgh, PA

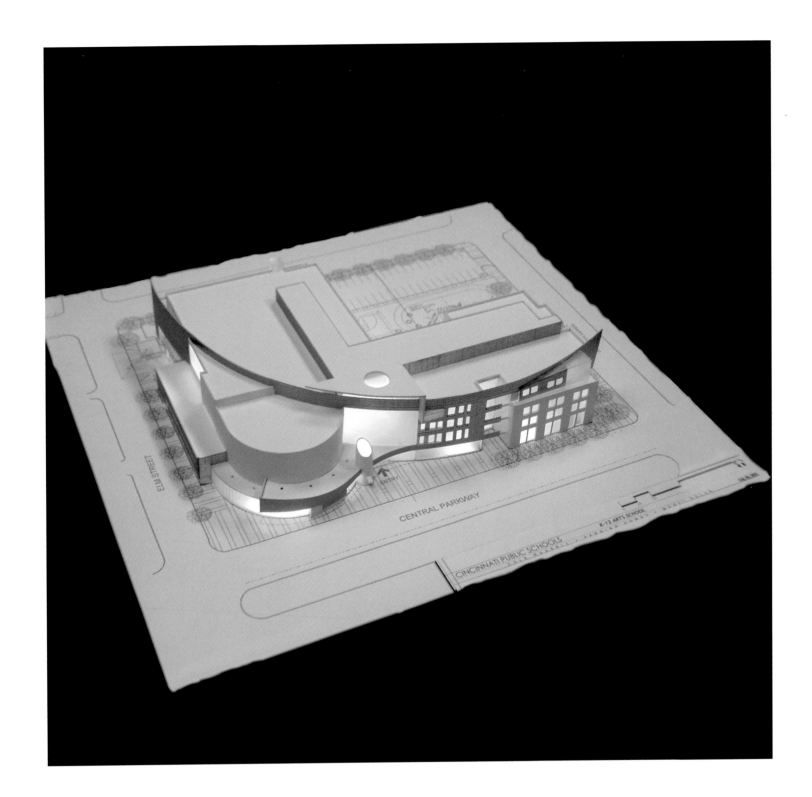

Cincinnati Public Schools
School for Creative and
Performing Arts (SCPA)
Cincinnati, OH

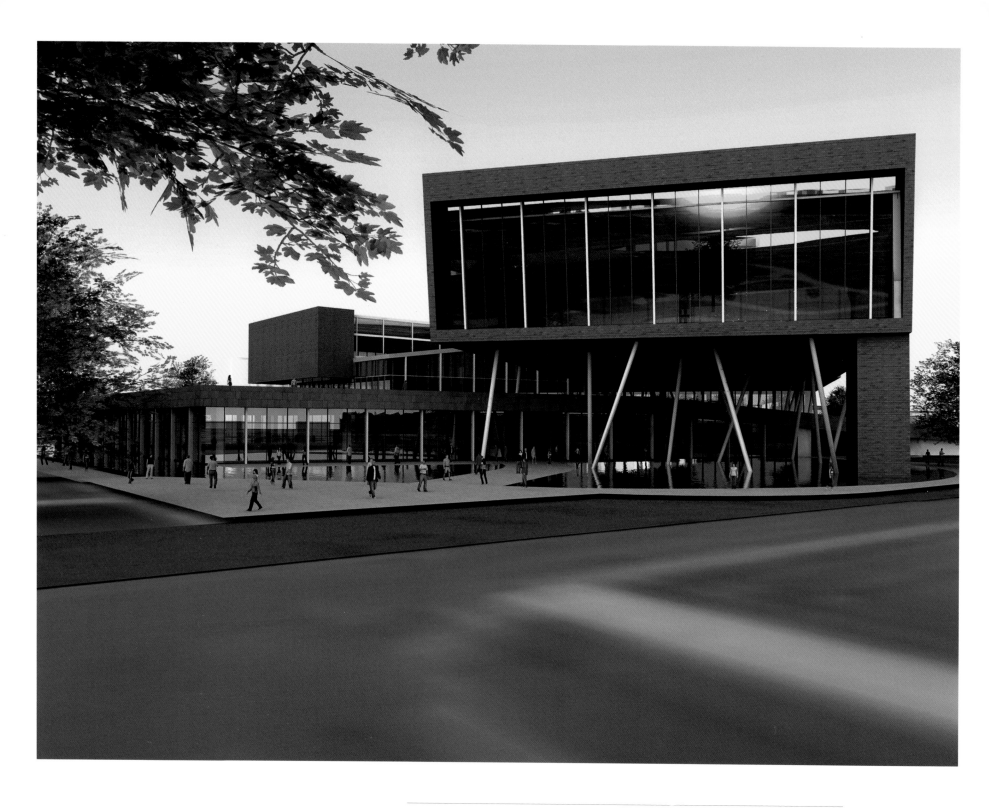

Ohio Northern University
McIntosh Student Center
Ada, OH

buildings — the dome or pinnacle, the main body of the building, and its arms — were an analogy to the recalling the inter-relationship of head, torso and limbs in the human body. Modernism, however, with its insistence on abstraction, largely disallowed the human body, at least in its literal form, from architecture.

Moody·Nolan is an essentially Modernist firm and has never used statuary. Still, the firm has repeatedly found ways to introduce the human body, and with it human scale, back into present-day architecture. One purpose in putting people on the façade of buildings is pragmatic, and refers back to the idea of communicating the way buildings are organized. There is a more immediate reason for including the sight of human beings in the elevation, however, people are always warmed by the sight of other people, and reintroducing people into building fronts seems like a way of giving the building an extra helping of humanity.

Another notable example of integrating people into buildings is the elevation of the Wayne T. and Mary T. Hockmeyer Hall at Purdue University in West Lafayette, Ind. Like the WSU Student Center, this building integrates outdoor walkways on the front of the building, and this device activates the building with the movement of students and faculty, while lending human scale to the elevation. As mentioned earlier, many of the surrounding science buildings on Purdue's life-sciences campus have very little glazing, so the exterior walkways on the second and third levels of Hockmeyer Hall seem to express the unconscious urge of students to escape their windowless warrens and breathe fresh air. In this case, both people inside the building, as well as those outside, may be refreshed by the presence of walkways on the façade.

Ohio Northern University
McIntosh Student Center
Ada, OH

Chapter 6

DETAILS

The detail—that is, the way that individual elements in architecture fit together—is the measure of craftsmanship in the art of building. This artfulness is more obvious in some cases than in others. In the case of Moody·Nolan's major buildings with budgets large enough to allow for fine materials, those kinds of detail are easy to discern. The steel shingles cladding the auditorium of the School for Creative and Performing Arts in Cincinnati, the metal soffit and ceiling at New Athletics and Events Center at Ithaca College in Ithaca, New York, and the curved steel-and-glass curtain wall for the Pittsburgh African American Cultural Center are all elaborate, in some cases, almost flamboyant, uses of fine materials. Even in a modest project like the Linden branch library in Columbus, Ohio, the sub-

Hampton University
Student Center
Hampton, VA

tle use of seemingly modest details helps lift a workaday project out of the realm of the ordinary.

Detail can serve purposes beyond mere décor, such as helping to explain the relationship of a building to its natural setting. At Ithaca College, Moody·Nolan specified the use of a tannish stone for the front walkway that leads into the building, and continues inside the building lobby and throughout the ground level. It happens that the building sits on bedrock made up largely of the same stone; a natural outcropping of the same stone can be found near the rear elevation of the building. By using the stone in the entrance sequence, Moody·Nolan makes the building look and feel embedded in the natural environment of the campus.

Another material which relates to its environment is brick, in cases where the environments are man-made and Midwestern. Brick walls help the colorful School for Creative and Performing Arts make friends with existing, inner-city buildings in downtown Cincinnati, as if to signal to visitors that we are looking at a new building that is aware of its surroundings. The brick surfaces at the school are not only contextual with the surrounding buildings, but might also be seen as protective camouflage for the colorful front elevation of the building. In Columbus' Arena District, the use of brick on the façades of the Nationwide Mutual Insurance Company Parking Garage helps identify the building with the city's downtown area, where brick is the most common material.

A virtuosic use of brick can be found at Baker University Center at Ohio University's Athens campus. As we saw earlier, this is a Janus-faced building, with a two-story, historicist façade on one side, and a five-story retail and administrative building on the other. To make the five-story portion of Baker compatible with the smaller, Colonial-styled building, Moody·Nolan has formulated a new style which could be called "contemporary college Georgian." This style is intended to recall historical detail while acknowledging that the five-story complex is a fully contemporary,

Ohio University
Baker University Center
Athens, OH

 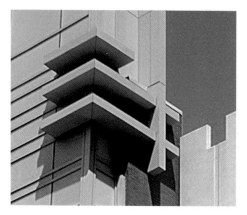 

Previous Page
**Nationwide Mutual
Insurance Company
Parking Garage**
Columbus, OH

technologically up-to-date building. The front elevation of the five-story building uses a range of historical-looking details—squared dormer windows, a brick wall with narrows, shallow stone arches and a pergola—that outwardly look historical but is actually a dynamic, contemporary Moody·Nolan elevation—assymetrical, sculptural, and dynamic in feeling. These features reveal that Baker is a modern building, more closely related to buildings like the Wayne State University Student Center in Detroit or the School for Creative and Performing Arts in Cincinnati than to Monticello.

The metal details on the exterior of the Linden branch library in Columbus may not seem extraordinary at first glance, but they add much of the style and charm alike to this neighborhood-scale building. Moody·Nolan designed the roof to resemble a sheet of folded metal, while metal sunshades reach outward from the west and south sides of the façade, each shielding a row of windows at the ground level. To make a visual connection between the roof and the sunshades, the architects introduced a set of metal cables, that appear to hold up the sun shades. In actuality, the cables are purely ornamental, because the roof does not actually support the weight of the metal shades. Instead, cables add a much-needed rhythm of vertical lines to the largely horizontal façade. The sunshades also serve as pedestals for rows of free-standing, supergraphic-style aluminum letters that identify the building simply as LIBRARY on the south and west elevations. The solitary word is a sophisticated and understated piece of signage that Robert Venturi, who has done much to re-integrate lettering back into architecture, would undoubtedly enjoy.

Frank Gehry has demonstrated the sculptural possibilities of glass in the IAC/InterActiveCorp headquarters in Manhatten; Moody·Nolan has been using glass in a similarly innovative way for some time. Glass, in fact, is probably the medium of the firm's most inventive effects. In the hands of Moody·Nolan's architects, glass refuses to stand still or lie flat. Instead, the

Columbus Metropolitan Library
Linden Branch Library
Columbus, OH

Harrisburg National Museum
of African American History
Design Competition
Harrisburg, PA

brittle, transparent material wants to become a three-dimensional object. The glass curtain wall in front of the Harrisburg National Museum of African American History in Pennsylvania seems to be in a state of metamorphosis before our eyes, turning from a flat sheet into a set of sliding, folded planes. At Hockmeyer Hall at Purdue, we have seen how the glass walls lining the front courtyard push outward, to become three-dimensional walkways; the glass seems to lunge forward, as if it were trying to escape the building. And in the Pittsburgh African American Cultural Center, glass curves and twists, changing from a wall to a roof and back again with the elasticity of bent metal.

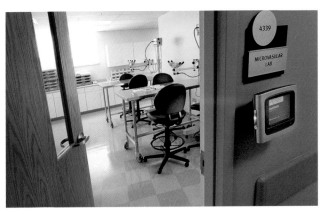

Riverside Methodist Hospital
Center for Medical Education
and Innovation™
Columbus, OH

Left
Akron Public Schools Barber Community Learning Center
Akron, OH

Above
Moody·Nolan's innovation has been to use the everyday materials of commercial construction to create a poetic metaphor for architecture, an art that is concerned simultaneously with the relationship of inner and outer.

Chapter 7

EPILOGUE

Mastery in architecture comes only after long experience. The typical career path of a good architect starts with a number of small projects wherein the fledgling designer works out a series of knotty formal and technical problems. Then a series of larger projects follow, in which the architect learns about how materials actually look in the sun and rain and overcast skies, and this is learned only after many trials. Scale—meaning the way buildings and spaces of varying sizes actually feel to human beings who walk on the ground and see the world from a height of five to seven feet—is probably the most difficult to learn and "get right."

Architects must also master technology. With a universe of materials and the mushrooming growth of technological and environmental issues—mechanical systems heating-cooling-ventilation, electrical and information systems, and now green-building standards—present-day architecture is arguably more difficult to master than the academic architecture of 100 years ago. In fact, the knowledge base of modern architecture has become so broad than almost no single individual can master all of it.

Fort Negley Visitors Center
Nashville, TN

Ohio Dominican University
Bishop James A. Griffin
Student Center
Columbus, OH

Mastery in architecture occurs only when the technical requirements converge with the artistic. In architecture that convergence tends to happen not earlier than mid-career and afterwards. In architecture, as much as any field in the arts, "ripeness is all," as a famous playwright once said.

All this is prelude to the most recent chapter in the career of Moody·Nolan, in which the experience of Curt Moody and his staff of 170 has resulted in a series of buildings that exult in the hard-won artistic maturity of the firm. As with any other seasoned firm, Moody·Nolan has identified a series of themes or strategies that the firm continues to explore, with increasing boldness, depth and conviction. The firm has attained to a kind of mastery, and with mastery comes confidence, versatility, and freedom.

Perhaps no building better illustrates the virtuosity of Moody·Nolan's recent work than the extraordinary spiral plan of the Ohio Northern

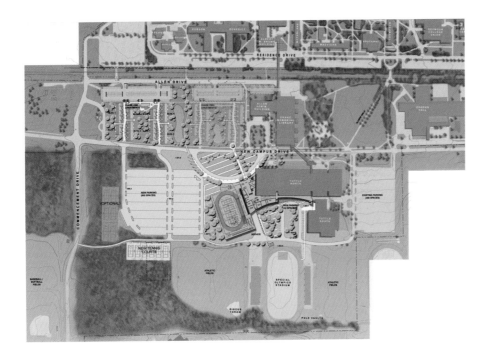

SUNY Brockport
Special Events/
Recreation Center
Brockport, NY

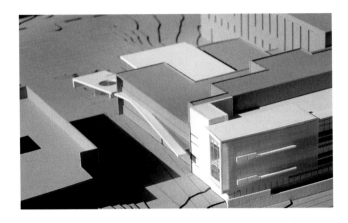

University McIntosh Student Center in Ada, Ohio. Green building is the theme of this unique design ("mining the earth to power the building" was the unofficial slogan) which incorporates co-generation, and makes drama out of a grassy ramp that stretches halfway around the building. Like several earlier designs (in Ithaca, New York and Athens, Ohio,) the Ohio Northern building operates on multiple ground planes. The start of our spiral journey begins on campus, where a gentle slope leads us to the second floor and the glass shed that serves as the second-story building entrance and access to ballrooms. The upper levels of the buildings complete the twist of the spiral, with the main volume of the building twisting 45 degrees from the original direction of the ramp. The playfully spindly, "crazy-leg" pylons beneath the big, overlapping volume may be an affectionate nod to Will Alsop's Sharpe Centre in Toronto.

Context, in both urban and campus design, is an operational principle at Moody·Nolan. At Purdue University in West Lafayette, Indiana, the addition to the Mechanical Engineering Building shows respect to the original, classical-style structure. Leaving the old building untouched, the new addition wraps itself around the historic structure, leaving a green path between the two. At SUNY Brockport Special Events/Recreation Center in Brockport, New York, the firm has covered over an insensitive, brutalist-style building from the 1970s with an outward-curving, glass-walled building that serves as a kind of "billboard" for students entering the campus from the west. Context here focuses on the contours of neighboring buildings: The curving footprint of the new addition parallels exactly that of an existing building to the immediate north, forming a clear path between the two. This is very similar to the way the S-shaped footprint of the Tom Muehlenbeck Center in Plano, Texas echoes the bend in the nearby river, and provides a walkway between the building and the water. So harmonious, in fact, is Moody·Nolan's addition to the Brockport building that the addition looks as if it had been designed with the surrounding buildings as a single, unified scheme.

Ohio Northern University
McIntosh Student Center
Ada, OH

Lentz Public Health Center
Renovation and Addition
Nashville, TN

Slippery Rock University
Student Union
Design Competition
Slippery Rock, PA

Contextuality is also in evidence at the Ohio Dominican University Bishop James A. Griffin Student Center, in Columbus, where the layout and internal circulation of the new building follow the multi-directional pattern of surrounding streets. Located across a busy street from the main campus, the interior spaces of the addition display both the transparency and the restless, energetic character we saw earlier in The Ohio State University Ohio Union. To accommodate students on foot, Moody•Nolan provides a new pedestrian bridge across the street. Landscape also counts: With a limited budget for glass, the architects concentrated the glazing toward south and west, to maximize the view of a wooded ravine—another example of the firm's ongoing attempt to bring landscape views into large buildings.

The knowledge that Moody•Nolan has acquired in designing its many student centers extends beyond the confines of the college campus and enters the life of the inner city with the Lentz Public Health Center renovation and addition in Nashville, Tennessee. More than merely adding an addition, the firm has completely re-imagined the way this public health facility works. The addition wraps around two existing buildings, creating a single, L-shaped complex. Taking a cue from airport design, the designers have created a long, concourse-like hallway, with clear signage. The public clinics occupy the sunny, outward-looking parts of the building, while the administrative offices are tucked into the more shadowy, inward-looking parts of the building facing the parking lot. Recognizing that the people generally enter the building from the parking lot, the firm re-oriented the entrance toward the rear of the building that takes visitors through a hallway to a central lobby. This clarity and simplicity of organization stands in contrast to the labyrinthine hallways found in many medical centers that grow by successive additions. Another example of unifying old buildings with a wraparound façade can be found in a design for the

The Banks Phase 1A
Cincinnati, OH

Slippery Rock University Student Union in Slippery Rock, Pennsylvania. Faced with two uninspired buildings from the 1970s, Moody·Nolan enlarged the student center with a façade that unites two existing box-like volumes with a simple curving elevation.

Civic-scale projects are prize challenges that have the potential to affect the lives not only of people who live and work in a particular building or complex, but the life of a city as a whole. Accordingly, these projects carry a big responsibility, because they will likely shape the behavior of city residents, to some degree, for several generations. In these "city-building" projects, Moody·Nolan's humane values remain at center stage.

City building often starts with the revamping of outmoded or unsuccessful buildings. In the case of the design of the City Center Redevelopment, also in Columbus, a failed, inward-looking shopping center becomes an extrovert, even flamboyant, mixed-use complex. The original "big box" of the old mall becomes a transparent glass box, its inner steel structure visible to the street. This box becomes the plinth (i.e. street-level platform) for a high-rise building in various shades of blue glass. This highly sculptural tower is one of the most daring designs to come out of Moody·Nolan. In an acknowledgement to the European trend to introduce greenery into façades, planting and even mature trees will be visible from mid-height of this twisting, torqueing tower. The bewildering range of activity proposed within this mixed-use building (one is tempted to call it "universal use") includes low-rise condos, big-box retail, an elevated park and waterfall, a child-care center, even a golf driving range, all above several floors of parking – recalls the megastructure fantasies of the 1960s. As in the megastructures, this mixed-use center is a self-contained, vertical city in itself.

A more conventional if no less interesting redevelopment project is Block 76 in downtown Kansas City, Missouri. Here some obsolete office

The Banks Phase 1A
Cincinnati, OH

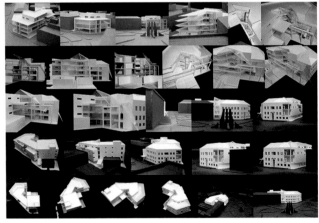

Purdue University
Mechanical Engineering
Building Addition
West Lafayette, IN

buildings become the starting point for an entire U-shaped block that combines new and old construction, all of it given a new wrap-around façade by Moody•Nolan. As in some earlier projects (the student center in Athens) the firm has explored ways to find modern-day equivalents of historical styles, without replicating them literally. The Kansas City elevations may be the firm's most successful essay yet in devising a crypto-historical style for a historic context.

The civic design with possibly the greatest potential impact is that of the The Banks in Cincinnati, which will create a unified waterfront between the Bengals stadium to the West and the Reds baseball field to the East. Proposed in an area that currently serves as a parking lot, The Banks Phase 1A introduces housing and infill retail buildings to the riverfront, while contributing an active, linear park between two of the city's biggest draws.

This book began with a description of a museum that lost a competition, and concludes with a competition winner. The future International African American Museum in Charleston, South Carolina, emphasizes the central role of the Carolinas in the slave trade of the 18th century and early 19th century, when this spot on the eastern seaboard formed one point in a triangle connecting the Americas with the western coast of Africa and an intermediate ports-of-call in the Caribbean. Working in collaboration with architect Antoine Predock, much of the museum will be devoted to documenting the role of the Carolinas as the port of entry for the majority of slave ships destined for North America. Given Moody•Nolan's ability to shape buildings around ideas, we can safely expect a powerful evocation of this blood-chilling event in American history.

**University of
Wisconsin–Madison
Union Redevelopment**
Madison, WI

Block 76
Feasibility Study
Kansas City, MO

Moody·Nolan's recent production confirms the firm's commitment to humane values, which might be defined as concerned with end user's quality of experience. Even in projects with bold architectural gestures, the basic value system of accommodating human beings remains down to earth. These values are of long standing. Even in the early days, when Moody·Nolan survived on routine assignments with Spartan budgets, the firm refused to go into default mode and ignore the people who will spend many hours, in some cases much of their lives, inside their buildings. While many of the firm's buildings look good in photographs, I suspect the firm does not design for the camera but rather for the student entering the Kress Events Center at the University of Wisconsin-Green Bay or perhaps a graduate student trying to find her way through the Structural Biology Building at Purdue University for the first time. During the firm's ascent into artistic mastery, this concern for wayfinding, the optimization of landscape and public space, the emphasis on improving places rather than merely overpowering them, have all remained constants in Moody·Nolan's work. And this attention to the human element is one good reason why the firm seems likely to hold our attention, and to improve many of our cities and college campuses, for years to come.

City Center Redevelopment
Columbus, OH

BalletMet Academy
Conceptual Design
Columbus, OH

IN COLLABORATION

**University of Illinois
at Chicago West Campus
Sports & Fitness Facility**
Design Architect: Moody•Nolan
Architect of Record: PSA Dewberry

**The Ohio State University
Recreation and Physical Activity
Center (RPAC)**
Design Architect:
Antoine Predock Architect PC
Architect of Record: Moody•Nolan

Tom Muehlenbeck Center
Design Architect: Moody•Nolan
Architect of Record:
Brinkley Sargent

**Youngstown City Schools
East High School**
Design Architect: Moody•Nolan
Architect of Record: Ricciuti Balog &
Partners Architects

**Ohio University
Baker University Center**
Architect of Record: Moody•Nolan
Associate Architect: WTW Architects

**Cincinnati Public Schools
School for Creative
and Performing Arts (SCPA)**
Architect of Record: Cole+Russell
Architects
Design Architect/Associate Architect:
Moody•Nolan
MEP/Landscape Architect:
Fanning/Howey

**Jackson State University
Student Center**
Architect of Record: Moody•Nolan
Associate Architect:
Barranco Architecture

**University of Wisconsin–Green Bay
Kress Events Center**
Design Architect: Moody•Nolan
Architect of Record:
Venture Architects

**Purdue University
Wayne T. and
Mary T. Hockmeyer Hall**
Design Architect: Moody•Nolan
Architect of Record:
URS Corporation

**Wayne State University
Student Center**
Design Architect/
Architect of Record: Moody•Nolan
Local Architect:
Partners in Architecture, PLC

**St. Elizabeth Hospital
Boardman Campus**
Associate Architect: Moody•Nolan
Architect of Record:
Strollo Architects

**University of Akron
Student Recreation
Center & Field House**
Architect of Record: Moody•Nolan
Associate Architect:
TC Architects, Inc.

**University of Wisconsin–River Falls
University Center**
Associate Architect: Moody•Nolan
Architect of Record:
Workshop Architects, Inc.

**University of Illinois
at Chicago East Campus
Student Recreation Facility**
Planning Consultant: Moody•Nolan
Architect of Record: PSA Dewberry

**SUNY Brockport
Special Events/Recreation Center**
Design Architect: Moody•Nolan
Architect of Record:
King & King Architects LLP

The Banks Phase 1A
Design Architect: Moody•Nolan
Architect of Record:
Cole+Russell Architects

**Purdue University
Mechanical Engineering
Building Addition**
Design Architect: Moody•Nolan
Architect of Record:
Scholer Corporation

**University of Wisconsin–Madison
Union Redevelopment**
Associate Architect: Moody•Nolan
Architect of Record:
Workshop Architects, Inc.

CURTIS J. MOODY, FAIA

Although today Moody·Nolan, Inc. is the largest African American owned architectural firm in the nation, that distinction did not come without its challenges. Founder Curtis J. Moody, FAIA, NCARB, had to overcome the obstacles of racial and financial prejudices to realize his dream of becoming an architect and leading his own firm.

Moody's passion for architecture began in the seventh grade when he experimented with designing houses that he admired in various magazines. Growing up, he also had a passion for sports. His determination to excel at both passions led him to win design competitions for houses at the local state fair while also winning accolades for his athletic abilities in basketball, track, football and baseball throughout school. Although it was clear to Moody's instructors and coaches that he was talented in both areas, the school counselor did not feel that there was a place for African Americans in the architecture field and advised him against pursuing architecture as a career. Nonetheless, Moody was determined to follow his dream.

The pursuit of this dream was further complicated when he received athletic scholarships to several universities that did not offer architecture as a major, which forced him to decide between a scholarship and architecture. Rather than give up on his dream of becoming an architect, Moody enrolled in the architectural program at The Ohio State University. Luckily, he didn't have to give up on his passion for athletics either and became a walk-on athlete on the university's varsity basketball team. He later earned a grant that helped fund his college education.

Upon graduating, Moody worked for local firms before founding Moody and Associates in 1982. The firm consisted of Moody and a graduate architect who served as secretary and office manager. But being a small firm was not the only challenge. The highly competitive architec-

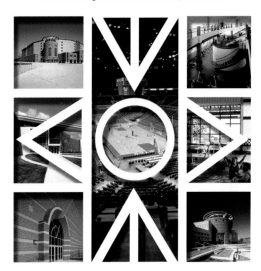

NOMA
National Organization of Minority Architects

Firm of the Year Winner
2000-2001
MOODY·NOLAN, INC.

National Organization of
Minority Architects Firm of
the Year Award

tural market was often unkind to minority firms due to the many societal misconceptions in the 1980s. At that time, minority architects were employed mostly in support roles and consequently there were few minority-owned firms of size and capability. But Moody was determined to overcome these challenges and win projects in which his firm had a leadership role. By the end of the first year of business, the firm had grown to nine staff members. Then, in 1984, Moody joined forces with the civil engineering firm of Howard E. Nolan, PE, which better positioned both firms for success.

Today, with a staff of 170, Moody·Nolan is headquartered in Columbus, Ohio, with offices in Cleveland, Ohio; Covington, Kentucky; Indianapolis, Indiana; Kansas City, Missouri; Nashville, Tennessee and Washington, DC. The firm offers services in architecture, interior design and civil engineering. Through the years, Moody·Nolan has been the lead designer and principal architect on some of the largest projects on college campuses throughout the U.S., including the $153 million Recreation and Physical Activity Center (RPAC) at The Ohio State University and the $45 million Baker University Center at Ohio University. Outside the collegiate arena, Moody·Nolan has led projects exceeding $70 million at Port Columbus International Airport as well as several other civic projects throughout Columbus.

Due to Moody's challenges pursuing a career in architecture and his belief that service and success are intertwined, he remains active in numerous associations, not only within the architecture industry, but the community as well. Moody has contributed professional expertise to the boards and executive management of more than 20 civic, banking, medical, minority, education, arts and professional groups, including Easter Seals, The Ohio State University School of Architecture Alumni Board of Governors, Columbus Area Chamber of Commerce and the Governor's Residence Advisory Commission. Influential community service roles

Curtis J. Moody Receiving the
Whitney M. Young, Jr. Award

have been performed through AmeriFlora, an international exposition in Columbus, Ohio, and the 1996 Olympics in Atlanta, Georgia.

In 1992, Moody was awarded the national Whitney M. Young, Jr. Award given to the outstanding minority architect by the American Institute of Architects, Washington, DC. His achievements include more than a dozen community service, business and minority leadership awards, including the prestigious Ernst & Young Entrepreneur of the Year Award in the Service Category, the Governor's Minority Business Award and the Urban League's Community Achievement Award, plus more than 125 local, state and national design citations.

Under Moody's leadership, Moody·Nolan has experienced great success, including being cited for more design accomplishments than any other African American design firm in the United States. In recent years, Moody·Nolan has captured over 25 design awards from the National Organization of Minority Architects (NOMA), more than any other African American firm in the nation. Civic and business leaders affirmed their confidence in Moody·Nolan by selecting them as the recipient of the Consumers' Choice Award™ for Business Excellence. Moody·Nolan was among the first firms selected in Columbus and the first architectural firm so designated in the United States. The firm is also the first to achieve this notoriety four consecutive years—2001, 2002, 2003, 2004, 2006 and 2007. Moody·Nolan was also recognized by AIA Ohio as the Gold Medal Firm of the Year for 2006, followed by Moody attaining the AIA Ohio Gold Medal Award in 2007 for his contributions to the architectural profession.

Above
Curtis J. Moody Featured in Ebony Magazine, Oct. 2005

Below
Curtis J. Moody at his FAIA Fellowship Induction Ceremony

Above
Board of Directors
From Left:
Elaine Moody;
Kathy Ransier;
Eileen M. Goodman, NCIDQ;
Robert K. Larrimer, AIA;
Curtis J. Moody, FAIA;
Arthur N. Cox, AIA;
Howard E. Nolan, PE

Below
Firm Principals
From Left:
Curtis J. Moody, FAIA, NCARB;
Robert K. Larrimer, AIA;
John S. Ensign, PE;
Paul F. Pryor, AIA, NCARB;
J. William Miller, AIA,
    ACHA, NCARB;

Eileen M. Goodman, NCIDQ;
Mark J. Bodien, AIA, LEED AP;
Elizabeth A. Thompson, AIA;
Donald Gardner, AIA, NCARB;
Howard E. Nolan, PE

PHOTOGRAPHER CREDITS /ACKNOWLEDGEMENTS

**University of Illinois
at Chicago West Campus Sports &
Fitness Facility**
Page 4, 70-71
Mark Ballogg, Steinkamp/Ballogg
Photography

**The Ohio State University
Recreation and Physical Activity
Center (RPAC)**
Page 7, 8, 65
Michael Houghton, StudiOhio

Page 56, 64
Brad Feinknopf, Feinknopf, LLC

Page 60-61
Tim Hursley

Tom Muehlenbeck Center
Page, 9, 12-13, 14
Charles Davis Smith, AIA

**Youngstown City Schools
East High School**
Page 10
Michael Houghton, StudiOhio

**Ohio University
Baker University Center**
Page 11, 54, 55, 57, 88
Brad Feinknopf, Feinknopf, LLC

**Jackson State University
Student Center**
Page 18, 32
Shannon Sheridan

**Smith Brothers
Hardware Renovation**
Page 19
Chun Y Lai Photography

**Nationwide Mutual
Insurance Company
Parking Garage**
Page 21
Brad Feinknopf, Feinknopf, LLC

Page 89
Michael Houghton, StudiOhio

**University of
Wisconsin–Green Bay
Kress Events Center**

Page 25, 26-27, 46, 75
Nels Akerlund, Nels Akerlund
Photography

Columbus Police Academy
Page 28, 29
Michael Houghton, StudiOhio

**Columbus State
Community College
Discovery Exchange**
Page 38, 39
Brad Feinknopf, Feinknopf, LLC

**University Hospitals
Twinsburg Health Center**
Page 40, 41
Michael Houghton, StudiOhio

**St. Elizabeth Hospital
Boardman Campus**
Page 42, 43 (top)
J. William Miller, AIA,
ACHA, NCARB

Page 43 (bottom)
William Webb, Infinity Studios

**The Ohio State University
at Marion
Library and Classroom Building**
Page 44, 47, 50-51
Owen Smithers, Leslee Kass

**University of Akron
Student Recreation
Center & Field House**
Page 48-49, 72, 73
Michael Houghton, StudiOhio

**Hampton University
Student Center**
Page 52, 53, 86
Michael Houghton, StudiOhio

**University of Wisconsin–River Falls
University Center**
Page 58, 59
Mark Heffron

**University of Illinois at Chicago
East Campus Student
Recreation Facility**
Page 68, 69

Mark Ballogg, Steinkamp/Ballogg
Photography

**Time Warner Cable
Mid-Ohio Division**
Page 78, 79
Eric Wagner, Illumination LLC

**Columbus Metropolitan Library
Linden Branch Library**
Page 92-93
Michael Houghton, StudiOhio

**Riverside Methodist Hospital
Center for Medical Education
and Innovation™**
Page 95
Michael Houghton, StudiOhio

Fort Negley Visitors Center
Page 98
Tom Gatlin, Tom Gatlin Photography

Curtis J. Moody, FAIA
Page 114, 118
Kevin Keefer

Board of Directors
Page 118
Rycus Associates Photography

**Paul F. Pryor, AIA, NCARB
Eileen M. Goodman, NCIDQ
Mark J. Bodien, AIA, LEED AP**
Page 118
Michael B. Smith /
three six one studios

Elizabeth A. Thompson, AIA
Page 118
Scott Totty

Donald Gardner, AIA, NCARB
Page 118
Jerry Lockett, Jerry Lockett
Photography